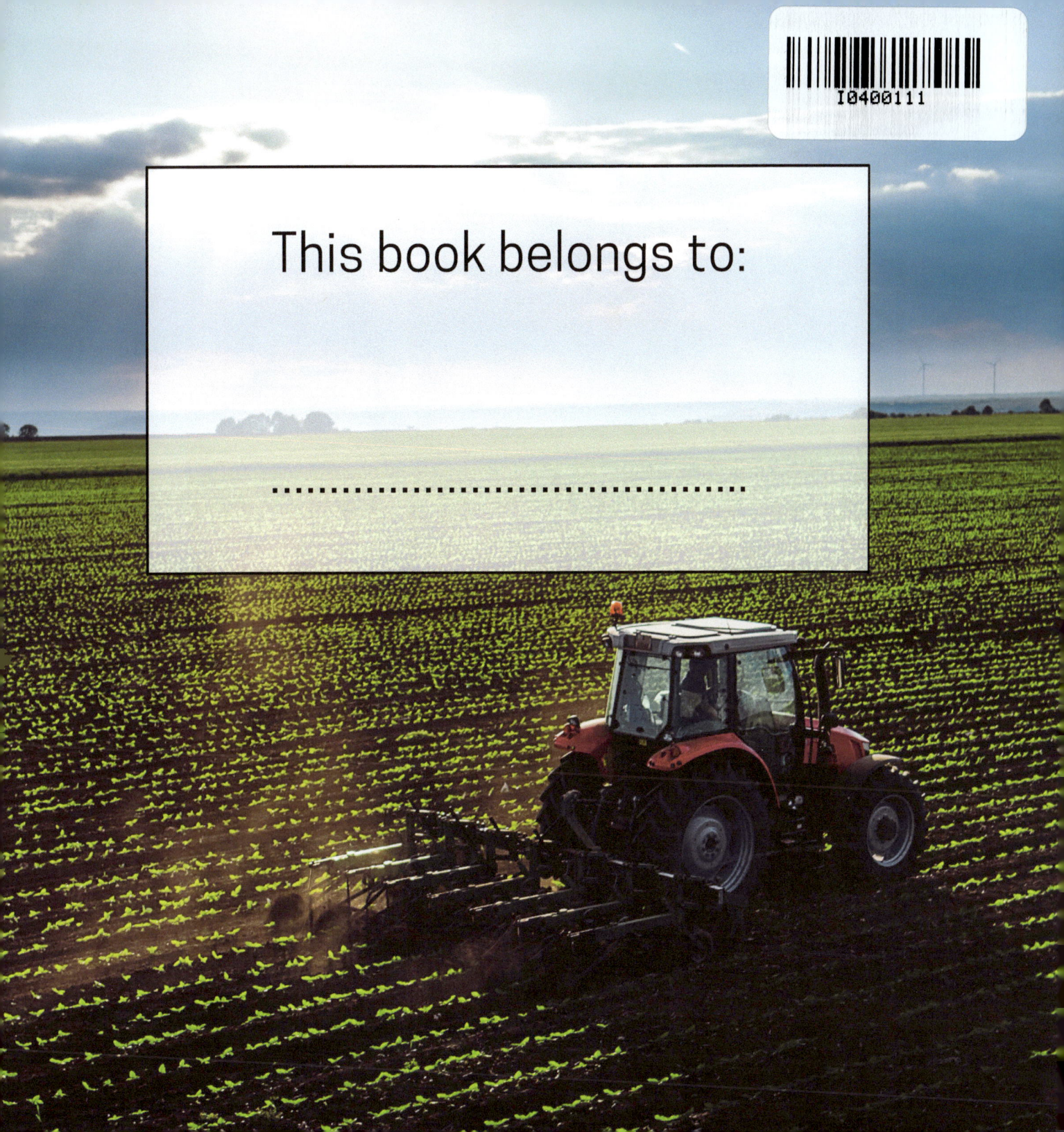
This book belongs to:
....

For my tractor loving son, Joshua.
- I.A. Blaikie

If you enjoy this book, please consider leaving a review. I am an independent author and this helps me tremendously. Thank you!

© I.A. Blaikie 2022

ISBN: 978-1-7397626-2-9

All rights reserved. No part of this book may be reproduced or distributed in any form without prior written permission from the author, with the exception of non-commercial uses permitted by copyright law.

The wheels on the tractor go round and round,

round and round,
round and round.

The wheels on the tractor go round and round, all through the farm.

The wipers on the tractor go
swish, swish, swish,

swish, swish, swish,
swish, swish, swish.

The wipers on the tractor go
swish, swish, swish, all through the farm.

The engine on the tractor goes chug, chug, chug,

chug, chug, chug,
chug, chug, chug.

The engine on the tractor goes
chug, chug, chug, all through the farm.

The farmer on the tractor goes "hum, hum, hum,

hum, hum, hum,
hum, hum, hum."

The farmer on the tractor goes "hum, hum, hum," all through the farm.

The lights on the tractor they shine, shine, shine,

shine, shine, shine,
shine, shine, shine.

The lights on the tractor they shine, shine, shine, all through the farm.

The trailer on the tractor goes rumble, rumble, rumble,

rumble, rumble, rumble,
rumble, rumble, rumble.

The trailer on the tractor goes rumble, rumble, rumble, all through the farm.

The plough on the tractor goes
dig, dig, dig,

dig, dig, dig,
dig, dig, dig.

The plough on the tractor goes
dig, dig, dig, all through the farm.

The seed drill on the tractor goes drill, drill, drill,

drill, drill, drill,
drill, drill, drill.

The seed drill on the tractor goes drill, drill, drill, all through the farm.

The loader on the tractor goes up and down,

up and down,
up and down.

The loader on the tractor goes up and down, all through the farm.

The end.

www.ingramcontent.com/pod-product-compliance
Lightning Source LLC
Chambersburg PA
CBHW040022130526
44590CB00036B/63